Contents Guide

Introduction

Old age is a time of life when many important changes have to be faced and decisions have to be made, sometimes in less than satisfactory circumstances. Many people will have to consider coming into contact with the helping services and may want to know their entitlement to help from this source in terms of domiciliary services, day care provision, respite care, or even just advice and information. Others may consider moving in with relatives and may need advice on their legal position when property is shared or transferred to the next generation. Deteriorating physical health may necessitate moving, perhaps to sheltered accommodation, maybe even into residential care. Planning and sorting out financial matters is an important task, whether it is retirement planning, making a will, or anticipating the situation where one may no longer be competent to manage one's own financial affairs.

With increasing life span and particularly the growth in number of the over-85s, it is important that the needs of this particular section of the community are addressed. One difficulty is that the law relating to the elderly is piecemeal and unco-ordinated. There is no single code of law relating to the elderly in our society such as there is with children. In any case, the actual needs of the elderly will vary widely from the 'active' elderly, which may include the majority of the 'young' elderly, the newly retired, to the group of the frail elderly where issues of vulnerability and disablement acquire greater prominence.

This book is intended as a guide to some of the more important legal issues particularly relevant to the needs of the elderly as a whole. It is aimed at professionals such as social workers, nurses and health visitors who come into day-to-day contact with older people as well as at older people themselves and their families and advisers.

The book is divided into four parts: services in the community, residential care, financial affairs, and death and family provision. The aim is to reflect a developmental view of old age with the emphasis on planning for change. The law, however, has a protective as well as an enabling function and must provide a solution in situations where the vulnerable elderly are clearly at risk in their present environment but are unwilling or unable to resolve their difficulties themselves. Thus the need for compulsory action, removal to hospital or to residential care, is also discussed and the implications for the elderly of the Mental Health Act 1983, are also examined.

In *Part One*, the focus is on the elderly as consumers of services such as home care, meals on wheels, day care, etc., which the local authority is empowered to provide through its social services department or which voluntary organisations also provide. Particular attention is paid to the needs of the disabled elderly in a critical examination of the Chronically Sick and Disabled Persons Act 1970 and the Disabled Persons Act 1986. The most important new development in this area is, of course, 'community care', and the implications for service-users of the National Health Service and Community Care Act 1990 are explained and discussed, with some caution however, as the new system will not be fully implemented until April 1993.

The resounding philosophy of the new Act and the White Paper, 'Caring for People', that preceded it is that it is preferable for people to be supported in the community for as long as possible. However, when this is no longer possible, residential care may have to be considered, and the various options of nursing home, private or voluntary residential home and local authority accommodation are discussed in *Part Two*. The legal distinctions between these types of care are explained, together with the registration requirements to which each type of home must conform. Some guidance is also given on the practicalities of moving into residential care, how to seek financial assistance with payment of fees and how to complain if the standard of care received is not satisfactory.

Dealing with financial matters is often a source of anxiety to elderly people and their relatives alike. *Part Three* looks at the range of state benefits which may be available and also discusses how to make use of one's existing financial assets in retirement. The problem of how to deal with financial matters when the elderly person himself is no longer capable of managing his own affairs, for whatever reason, is discussed. Legal devices do exist to deal with these situations, ranging from simple agency arrangements to the granting of ordinary and enduring powers of attorney. The role of the Court of Protection in dealing with the financial affairs of the mentally incapacitated elderly is often ill-understood; it is both more flexible and less difficult to deal with than the layman might think.

The theme of financial management is continued in *Part Four* which looks at the issue of family provision upon bereavement. The legal formalities connected with a death and the making of wills are explained. Family provision on intestacy is also discussed, as are the tax implications of various types of financial arrangements.

It is impossible to anticipate the whole range of complex issues which may arise in any of the areas covered by this book and further professional advice will be needed in interpreting the requirements of the law in individual cases. The legal system referred to throughout is that of England and Wales; Scotland and Northern Ireland have their own legal system. There are a number of organisations dealing with the elderly from which information may be sought, and a list of these is included in the *Appendix.* Suggestions for further reading are included at the end of each section for those who wish to take the discussion further.

Part One

Services in the Community

Successful care in the community means meeting an amalgam of housing, medical and personal care needs. The law generally performs an enabling function, allowing needs to be defined, resources to be provided and choices to be made. However, it also may perform a protective function when further assistance is needed.

Housing

Approximately 50% of older people are owner/occupiers, 40% are public sector tenants and 10% live in privately rented accommodation. This is a lower rate of owner-occupancy than for the general population. Across all categories of housing, low state of repair and lack of basic amenities are more prominent in housing occupied by older people. Grants for home improvements, which are mandatory in the case of standard amenities and in other cases discretionary, are governed by the Housing Act 1985. Adaptations of property to suit the needs of disabled people are available under the Chronically Sick and Disabled Persons Act 1970 (see below).

Sheltered accommodation, with or without resident warden services, is an increasingly popular option and a number of housing associations are specialists in this field. Some private sheltered accommodation is available. Very sheltered housing provides intensive personal care services as well as warden services.

A home is a major capital asset and tenants in the public sector were given 'the right to buy' by the Housing Act 1980. However, some types of dwelling are excluded from the right to buy: these include specially designed dwellings for physically handicapped people, and group sheltered accommodation for elderly people where special facilities are provided. Housing which is 'particularly suitable' for occupation by people of pensionable age by virtue of location or design may also be excluded on a discretionary basis.

Medical Care

General medical care under the National Health Service is available as a right to all UK residents. If registration with a GP poses difficulties, an approach should be made to the Local Family Practitioner Committee for allocation by them. Patients wishing to consult their doctor are normally expected to attend the surgery but a GP is required to attend a patient at their home if a patient's condition requires it; they are also required to provide 24-hour cover. There is no required frequency of visiting but the present funding structure for GP practices is such as to encourage preventative health care, in particular the offer of annual health checks to the over-75s. Community nursing services exist to provide medical assessment and care within the NHS; however, there is an increasing blurring of the boundaries between the tasks undertaken by such people as district nurses and home carers employed by the local authority. Whilst NHS services of this nature are free of charge, this is not necessarily the case with local authority services. The local authority may recover whatever charges it considers reasonable, except when satisfied that the user of a service has insufficient means; this is a matter of considerable contention in practice.

Seen positively, multi-disciplinary assessment and service delivery will be an important feature of care in the community as that concept is currently being developed.

Social Services

There are a number of services for elderly people which the local authority *has a duty* to provide and a larger number of services which the local authority merely *has a power* to provide. The breadth and type of service provision varies greatly from one part of the country to another.

Services that the local authority must provide

Residential Care

Part III of the National Assistance Act 1948 imposes a duty upon a local authority to provide residential accommodation "for persons aged 18 and over who by reasons of age, illness, disability, or any other circumstances are in need of care and attention which is not otherwise available to them". This duty is owed to those who are ordinarily resident within the area of the local authority and the accommodation thus provided is often referred to by its statutory title as 'Part III accommodation'.

Admission to residential care is dealt with in Part Two of this book. Admission, however, need not be on a permanent basis; a number of beds are usually set aside for what is known as 'short-term care' for simply a week or two weeks to provide respite or convalescence and this may be available on a regular basis.

Where a person is admitted as a patient to hospital, or to accommodation provided under Part III, then the local authority has a further duty to carry out what is known as a 'protection of property'. That means that the local authority has a duty to mitigate any loss or damage otherwise likely to be caused to that person's moveable property e.g. by theft or fire. This will be done by means of a witnessed inventory and, possibly, the removal of valuable items. Local authorities carry insurance to cover property protected in this way. There is a right of entry to premises to enable a protection of property to be carried out. Local authorities will also make arrangements for pets to be cared for during the owner's absence.

Domiciliary Services

Every local authority has a duty to provide a home help service 'on such a scale as is adequate for the needs of their area' for those who require help due to illness, handicap or age. This duty is now contained in Schedule 8 of the National Health Service Act 1977, which also gives a power to local authorities to provide laundry services where home help is being provided. The trend, however, is away from the provision of a home help service as such towards a home care service with the emphasis on personal care and support rather than domestic duties. Therefore, a home help service may not be available on request for cleaning alone and clients may well be directed towards private domestic agencies.

Services that the local authority may provide

Whilst the above are duties imposed by statute upon local authorities, the provision of other supportive services is discretionary insofar as statute provides only for a general power to promote the welfare of the elderly. The general power is contained in Section 45 of the Health Services and Public Health Act 1968 which provides that:

> *"A local authority may with the approval of the Secretary of State, and to such an extent as he may direct shall make arrangements for promoting the welfare of old people."*

Approval has subsequently been given for the setting up of meals on wheels and day care facilities (including the provision of any necessary transport), the development of 'boarding out' schemes for elderly people, the provision of visiting and advisory services and social work support, the provision of practical assistance in the home and for the adaptation of property, and the provision of warden services in public and private housing. Strictly speaking, any local authority scheme outside these parameters would need the specific approval of the Secretary of

State. However, no local authority is under a duty actually to provide any of these services.

Private day care services have yet to develop to any appreciable extent but where they do exist the local authority has inspection but not registration duties. It is the voluntary sector, e.g. Age Concern, the Salvation Army and Red Cross, which are most active in the field of day care and meals on wheels provision.

Again, what is available varies very much from one part of the country to another, so it is important for enquiries to be made locally about what services are provided and by whom.

Services for People with a Disability

The provision of services for disabled people is governed by the Chronically Sick and Disabled Persons Act 1970 and the Disabled Persons (Services, Consultation and Representation) Act 1986. Knowledge of these Acts is important for older people, since people over the age of 60 comprise approximately 60% of the disabled population as a whole.

The Chronically Sick and Disabled Persons Act 1970

This Act imposes a duty upon the local authority to assess the needs of disabled persons and to provide them with services. The term 'disabled' is wide enough to include those with chronic conditions such as bronchitis, diabetes and heart disease, as well as those suffering from mental disorder or handicap. Local authorities maintain registers of disabled people in their area but registration should not be a prerequisite for obtaining services. The services provided under the Chronically Sick and Disabled Persons Act are:

- domiciliary care
- the provision of meals within the home or elsewhere

- telephone installation (including the installation of special equipment) and the payment of telephone rental
- help with holidays
- the provision of recreational facilities outside the home and assistance with travel to those facilities
- aids and adaptations, e.g. ramps and showers
- the administration of the 'orange badge' scheme for disabled drivers.

Local authorities are required by the Act to inform themselves of the level of need within their area and to give information about services provided by them. Assessment is usually done by occupational therapists. However, levels of provision vary widely in different parts of the country. The courts have been reluctant to become involved in disputes between clients and local authorities about the adequacy of services under the Act, arguing that decisions concerning the allocation of services have been given by Parliament to the local authority, and that the only proper remedy for neglect of this duty lies in the default powers of the Secretary of State – in other words, a political solution. The first step to take now would be to use the local authority's own complaints procedure, which every local authority is required to have.

The Disabled Persons (Consultation and Representation) Act 1986

The Disabled Persons Act 1986 goes beyond the Chronically Sick and Disabled Persons Act 1970 in requiring local authorities to provide information not only about their own services but also about those services provided by other statutory and voluntary bodies concerned with disabled people. The Act also requires the needs of carers to be taken into account when the provision of services is being assessed. The 1986 Act requires the local authority to provide no new services; what the Act does however, is require that the local authority should develop a procedure which enables the views of the disabled person and their carers directly to be taken into account. To this end, Sections 1 to 3 of the Act provide for the appointment of advocates or 'representatives' to speak on behalf of those clients who are unable to express themselves directly. Section 3 of the Act furthermore requires the local authority to provide a written statement setting out the assessment of need. However, Sections 1 to 3 of the Act have not yet been brought into force, much to the dismay of organisations active on behalf of disabled people.

It should be noted that the Chronically Sick and Disabled Persons Act and the Disabled Persons Act apply to people who are resident in hospital and in residential and nursing homes as well as those who are living in the community. They are equally entitled to assessment and services from the local authority.

Elderly Mentally Infirm People

Elderly mentally infirm people pose particular problems of assessment, intervention and treatment. The issue is an important one because the prevalence of mental disorder in fact reaches a peak in later life. There is a high incidence of depression, often associated with changes in lifestyle or bereavement. But dementia, characterised by the decline of short-term memory and disorientation as to person or time, is seen as the classic mental illness of old age. The incidence of dementia is about 5% in the population over 65 and 20% in the population over 80 in England and Wales. Dementia is a progressive illness and legal mechanisms therefore need to be sensitive to the varying needs of people at different stages of their illness. The majority of people suffering from mental illness in old age are supported informally in the community by their GP, perhaps with access to services such as day centres and home care. Assessment by a consultant psycho-geriatrician will confirm the diagnosis and is the gateway to in-patient care or hospital day care. The law only really becomes important when the offer of services is refused, giving cause for concern for the patient's welfare, and the exercise of compulsion then needs to be considered.

The current legislation is the Mental Health Act 1983, supported by the Code of Practice under the Act published in May 1990. The Code of Practice is not law but is an aid to good practice in the interpretation of the Mental Health Act. There is also a watchdog body, the Mental Health Act Commission, which oversees the implementation of the Act and produces an annual report. The Mental Health Act itself sets out those circumstances in which compulsory admission to hospital for assessment or treatment may be authorised. Insofar as the interpretation of the Act is based almost entirely on professional discretion, it is an example of what may be called 'therapeutic law'. The professionals concerned are registered medical practitioners "authorised as having special training in the assessment and treatment of mental disorder" (these are consultant psychiatrists and also some GPs). Approved Social Workers (ASWs) are appointed by the local authority to introduce a social element into the assessment.

Section 131 of the Act, however, makes it clear that, for anyone over the age of sixteen years and capable of expressing his own wishes, informal admission should be the norm "and should be used whenever a patient is not unwilling to be admitted and can be treated without the use of compulsory powers". The term used is informal, not voluntary admission, the emphasis thus being on an absence of resistance rather than a positive giving of consent. The vast majority of admissions are in fact informal, particularly in the case of older people.

Compulsory Admission to Hospital under the Mental Health Act 1983

In all cases, application for admission (based on medical recommendation) can be made either by an ASW or by the patient's nearest relative. This process is commonly known as 'sectioning'. Most applications are by an ASW but the Mental Health Act Section 26 itself provides a hierarchy for deciding who is the 'nearest relative' in any case. This hierarchy is:

- Husband or wife of the patient (including cohabitees who have lived with the patient for more than six months)
- son or daughter
- father or mother
- brother or sister
- grandparent
- grandchild
- uncle or aunt
- niece or nephew

The 'nearest relative' is the person first described in this list, with the eldest in any category taking precedence, regardless of sex.

Central to the functioning of the Mental Health Act 1983 is the definition of 'mental disorder' in Section 1(2) of the Act; there are four specific forms of mental disorder: mental illness, arrested or incomplete development of mind, psychopathic disorder and 'any other disorder or disability of mind'.

The inclusion of 'arrested or incomplete development of mind' within the definition of mental disorder means that people with learning difficulties may come within some sections of the Mental Health Act. Promiscuity or other immoral conduct, sexual deviancy or dependence on drugs or alcohol do not in themselves constitute a mental disorder (Mental Health Act 1983 Section 1(3)). Mental illness is nowhere defined in the Act, nor have the courts given any real guidance as to its proper interpretation; its meaning therefore is a matter of clinical practice.

Admission for Assessment
Mental Health Act 1983 Section 2

The grounds are that the patient is suffering from mental disorder of a nature or degree which warrants his detention in a hospital for assessment (or for assessment followed by medical treatment) for a limited period of up to 28 days. An application for admission must be founded on the written recommendations of two medical practitioners, one of whom must be approved as having special experience in the diagnosis and treatment of mental disorder and one of whom should, if practicable, have had previous acquaintance with the patient. The applicant must have personally seen the patient within the previous 14 days and admission must take place within 14 days of the date of the second medical examination.

The nearest relative cannot prevent an application under Section 2 if made by an approved social worker, but can discharge the patient after 72 hours notice, subject to a bar by the responsible medical officer (RMO) on the grounds that the patient would be likely to act in a manner dangerous to himself or others.

Mental Health Act 1983 Section 4

Section 4 of the Mental Health Act 1983 contains a provision for emergency admission for assessment on the grounds that it is of urgent necessity for the patient to be admitted and detained under Section 2 (above) but that compliance with all the pro-cedural formalities would involve undesirable delay. Only one medical recommendation is needed and the doctor need not be approved; however he should, if practicable, have had previous acquaintance with the patient and must have seen him within the previous 24 hours from the time of admission to hospital. The authority to detain lapses after 72 hours unless it is 'converted' to a Section 2 admission by the giving of a second medical recommendation. There is no formal power of discharge or appeal in respect of emergency admission for assessment. It is argued that in some cases Section 4 powers are abused by being applied in non-emergency situations.

Admission for Treatment

Mental Health Act 1983 Section 3

Admission for treatment is a far more draconian power than admission for assessment since it involves the power to give treatment to a patient (subject to some limitations) without his consent. The period of detention is also longer, being for an initial (but renewable) period of up to six months. Such an application cannot be made by an approved social worker if the nearest relative (who should in any case be consulted) objects. An application for admission must be founded on the written recommendations of two medical practitioners. The classes of persons liable to be detained under Section 3 are also more limited. The patient must be suffering from mental illness, psychopathic disorder, severe mental impairment or mental impairment. Severe mental impairment and mental impairment must however be associated with 'abnormally aggressive or seriously irresponsible conduct'. There is also a 'treatability' test in the case of psychopathic disorder or mental impairment; that is: the treatment to be given upon admission should be such as is likely to alleviate or prevent a deterioration in his condition.

Powers of Entry and Powers of Detention

There may be circumstances in which entry to premises is being refused and legal powers need to be sought. These are contained in Section 115 and Section 135 of the Act.

Section 115 authorises an approved social worker to enter and inspect any premises which are not a hospital and in which a mentally disordered patient is living if he has reasonable cause to believe that the patient is not under proper care. It is an offence for anyone to obstruct him without reasonable cause (Section 129). Section 115, however, does not permit entry by force, nor does it contain any power of removal. For these latter purposes, a warrant under Section 135 of the Act authorising a police constable to make entry is needed.

Section 136 Mental Health Act 1983

Section 115 and Section 135 deal with persons found on private premises. However, Section 136 gives the police power to detain persons "who appear to be suffering from mental disorder and to be in immediate need of care and control" who are found in places "to which the public have access". Removal is to a 'place of safety', but must be "either in the interests of the person concerned or necessary for the protection of other people". No central records are kept of the use of this section but obviously the 72-hour period of detention authorised by Section 136 is capable of being used for *de facto* admission if the patient is taken directly to hospital by the police.

Guardianship

Guardianship is a legal device whereby a degree of formal control can be exercised over people who are suffering from mental disorder but who remain within the community. Its best use is in a supportive way to enable the provision of services which might otherwise be refused. Guardianship might also be used when elderly people in residential care are expressing a wish to leave in circumstances in which this would not be in their own best interests and informal persuasion is inadequate.

The grounds for reception into guardianship in civil cases are contained in Section 7(1) of the Mental Health Act 1983. The patient must be suffering from mental illness, psychopathic disorder, severe mental impairment or mental impairment of a nature or degree which warrants his reception into guardianship and it must be necessary in the interests of the welfare of the patient or for the protection of other persons that the patient should be so received. In contrast to the 1959 Mental Health Act which gave the guardian all the powers that a parent has over a child under the age of 14, the Mental Health Act 1983 limits the powers of the guardian to three particular instances: 1) to require the patient to reside at a place specified by the guardian; 2) to require the patient to attend for medical treatment, education or training; and 3) to require access to the patient to be given to any doctor, approved social worker or any other person similarly specified (Section 8(2)). It is the limited nature of these powers and the lack of any sanctions for their breach which is the main reason for guardianship's lack of popularity (less than 200 cases per year).

A private individual may be appointed guardian, but he must have the approval of his local social services authority so to act; in the majority of cases it will be the local authority that is appointed guardian. Guardianship lasts for an initial period of six months but may be renewed for a further six months and then for a year at a time. The local authority has visiting duties during the period of guardianship. It is particularly important to note that guardianship gives no authority over financial affairs; for that, a separate application will be needed to be made to the Court of Protection (see Part Three).

The Mental Health Review Tribunal

Mental Health Review Tribunals incorporate a quasi-judicial element into the law of mental health by providing a means by which appeal can be made against compulsory detention or the imposition of guardianship. Patients admitted for assessment can apply within the first 14 days of their admission and patients admitted for treatment or received into guardianship can apply during the first six months. If the nearest relative applies to discharge a patient under Section 3 and his application is blocked, he can appeal to the Mental Health Review Tribunal within 28 days of that application being blocked. There is also a procedure for the automatic review of all patients admitted for treatment under civil powers who have not exercised their right to apply within the first six months. Further reviews will be carried out at intervals of not less than three years.

There is a Tribunal for each of the separate health authority regions comprising of a legal chairman, a medical member and a lay person. The tribunal must sit in private to take evidence (unless the patient asks for it to be in public), usually at the hospital at which the patient is detained. There is no appeal from the decision of a Mental Health Review Tribunal, though, if a misinterpretation of its powers or procedural impropriety is alleged, there is the possibility of judicial review in the High Court.

After-Care Duties

Section 117 of the Mental Health Act 1983 imposes a duty on health and social services authorities to provide 'after-care' services for patients who have been detained for treatment. The type of services to be provided, however, are nowhere defined.

The Code of Practice suggests that discussions prior to discharge should take place between the hospital staff, social workers, the GP and the patient and/or a relative of his if he so wishes. The local authority's contribution to after-care (or indeed preventative work) may involve the use of the Mental Illness Specific Grant provided for in Section 50 of the National Health Service and Community Care Act 1990 to enable them to provide services for mentally ill people residing in their area.

Section 47 National Assistance Act 1948

Apart from the mental health legislation outlined above, there is no legal authority compulsorily to intervene in the lives of elderly people deemed to be at risk in the community except for Section 47 of the National Assistance Act 1948 and the National Assistance (Amendment) Act 1951. These two pieces of legislation, criticised as ageist in their conception, are used in perhaps 200 instances each year, but there is wide geographical variation in their use and in their interpretation.

Unlike compulsory admission to hospital under modern mental health legislation, compulsory removal from home under the National Assistance Act remains a judicial procedure, application being made to the local magistrates' court. Section 47 is directed to securing by compulsory removal to hospital or to residential care "the necessary care and attention" for persons who:

a) *are suffering from grave chronic disease or being aged, infirm or physically incapacitated are living in insanitary conditions and*

b) *are unable to devote to themselves and are not receiving from other persons proper care and attention.*

Therefore, being elderly and living in insanitary conditions and being unable (or unwilling) to receive proper care and attention is in itself a sufficient condition for removal from one's home for a period of up to three months. The procedure is that the local authority acts on the written recommendation of the community physician for the district (referred to in the section as the 'proper officer'). Most local authorities would convene a case conference before making such an application and it is the recommendation of the British Association of Social Workers that the authority should be satisfied that the physical, emotional and psychological wellbeing of the person would be improved by compulsory removal from their home given the distress that this involves. It is noteworthy however that Section 47 does not authorise compulsory medical treatment of any person thus removed. Cleaning up the premises would be dealt with under the public health legislation.

In an emergency, when the necessary seven days' notice to the patient required by Section 47(2) cannot be given, Section 1 of the National Assistance (Amendment) Act 1951 comes into play. Under the terms of the 1951 Act an *ex parte* application (i.e. an application without notice) can be made and to a single justice if necessary. However, two medical opinions are required under the emergency procedure and the period of detention is for three weeks, not three months. Local authorities may also authorise the community physician to make direct applications to the magistrates' court under the Act of 1951. The use of Section 47 should be considered very carefully: might it be more appropriate in any given situation to use the Mental Health Act (which has better procedural safeguards), and whose interests does it really serve, the patients or those of the community to whose standards he has chosen not to conform?

Abuse of the Elderly

A further situation in which individuals may be considered to be at risk, and one which is of growing concern, is that of abuse, either within the family or outside it or indeed in residential care. There is no authoritative definition of what constitutes abuse; suggested categories, however, are physical, sexual, emotional and financial abuse and neglect. The absence of any separate body of law relating to the elderly means that, in examining the issue of abuse, we must fall back upon general legal principles and remedies often developed in other contexts. Some parallels of course exist with child abuse but it cannot be assumed that similar rights and duties will exist, nor that similar remedies will be appropriate.

In the most extreme of situations, there is the criminal law, with the police, or in rare instances, private individuals bringing prosecutions for assault, indecent assault or theft as appropriate. One difficulty however may lie in obtaining sufficient reliable evidence from witnesses who may be mentally and physically infirm and who must attend court in person to give evidence, which must be on oath. Prosecuting institutional abuse within hospitals or residential homes may pose particular problems because of the uncorroborated nature of the evidence.

The domestic violence legislation, the Domestic Violence and Matrimonial Proceedings Act 1976 and the Domestic Proceedings and Magistrates' Courts Act 1978, can only be used between spouses or cohabitees where the appropriate remedies are the ousting of one party from the matrimonial home or an injunction or non-molestation order for the protection of the complainant spouse. An injunction is not available against other family members except as a corollary to an action for (often nominal) damages for, for example, trespass or assault. This is an instance of the use of the civil law where the initiative for taking action lies with the individual concerned. Those who are incapacitated from taking action on their own behalf may act through the Official Solicitor.

Cases of neglect, however, pose particular difficulties; in order to found a remedy in a case of neglect, it is first of all necessary to find a person who owes a duty to the elderly victim of that neglect. Whilst parents owe a duty to their infant children, children and other family members do not conversely owe a legal duty to elderly parents. It is otherwise if a duty is voluntarily assumed; civil liability will exist in the law of tort for the negligent breach of that duty and if there is gross negligence then there may well be criminal liability as well.

The standard of care that the courts have demanded has in fact been quite high and the greater the risks, the higher the standard of care. Constant supervision may thus be required, particularly in an institutional context, in the case of clients, such as the elderly mentally infirm, who present particular risks. If a duty of care is found to exist, then it is no defence for the defendant to say that he would have found it difficult because of his own limitations properly to fulfil that duty; the test is an objective one – what would a reasonable person in the circumstances have done?

A number of local authorities are drawing up procedural guidelines for dealing with allegations of abuse of the elderly. These exist independently of any legal remedies which may be available. Case conferences and 'at risk' registers on the child protection model may be features of these procedures. However the emphasis, throughout, must be on self-determination and the rights of older people to eschew protection from the state if they so wish.

The Impact of the National Health Service and Community Care Act 1990

At the time of writing, this is a period of uncertainty concerning the impact of the National Health Service and Community Care Act 1990. The Act gives substance to the government's plans for community care following the Griffiths' Report (1988) and the White Paper 'Caring for People: Community Care in the Next Decade and Beyond' (1989). The government's objectives stated in the White Paper are to develop new systems and procedures "designed to enable people to live an independent and dignified life at home, or elsewhere within the community, for as long as they are able and wish to do so".

In fact the Act imposes no new substantive duties on health authorities and local authorities to provide services that were not available before. Services such as domiciliary care, day care and meals on wheels are referred to in the Act as 'community care services'; what will change is the way in which these community care services are planned for, delivered and monitored. The Act is being introduced in stages up to April 1993, but it is anticipated that it may well take up to a decade beyond that for the new system to be fully operational.

The local authority is made the 'lead' authority in planning for community care services and by April 1992 was expected to have drawn up the first of its annual community care plans, following a wide-ranging consultation process to include the District Health Authority, the Family Health Services Authority, the local housing authority and "any such voluntary organisation as appears to the authority to represent the interests of persons who use or are likely to use any community care services within the area of the authority, or the interests of private carers who, within that area provide care for persons for whom, in the exercise of their social services functions, the local authority have a power or a duty to provide a service". The community care plan, once drawn up, becomes a public document.

The ethos of the government's policy is the development of what has been called a "mixed economy of care", with the local authority increasingly withdrawing from the direct provision of services and adopting an enabling role *vis-a-vis* the voluntary and private sector. The provision of services will be achieved by the drawing up of contracts between the voluntary and private sectors and the local authority. By April 1993, within the local authority there will be a clear division between the purchasers of care and providers of care which will permeate the whole management structure. Those who purchase care will be known as case managers; this is the role at present performed by the local authority social worker but it is envisaged that those outside the local authority structure, e.g. health visitors and community nurses, may also become case managers in their own right. There is a duty upon the local authority to provide an assessment of need when one is requested; such an assessment should take into account the needs of the carers as well as clients. There is also an emphasis on quality control, through contract specification and monitoring of standards by inspection units within the local authority. Replacing the previous *ad hoc* system of complaints procedures, there is a new duty upon all authorities to have a two-tier complaints procedure which conforms to a national standard. If complaints cannot be resolved internally by the local authority's own senior managers, reference is then made to a panel which includes a person who is entirely independent of the local authority. There is a plethora of official guidance on the implementation of the new system of community care published by the Department of Health and the Social Services Inspectorate. In future, central government will have a higher profile in ensuring standards are adhered to.

Suggestions for further reading

DOH (1988) "Community Care, Agenda for Action", (The Griffiths' Report), HMSO, London

DOH (1989) "Caring for People. Community Care in the Next Decade and Beyond" (The White Paper), HMSO, London

DOH (1990) "Community Care in the Next Decade and Beyond", (The Policy Guidance), HMSO, London

DOH (1992) "Implementing Community Care. Improving Independent Sector Involvement in Community Care Planning", HMSO, London

Marshall, M. (1990) "Social Work with Old People", Macmillan, Basingstoke

Age Concern (1986) "The Law and Vulnerable Elderly People", Age Concern, England

Griffiths, A., Grimes, R. & Roberts, G. (1990) "The Law and Elderly People", Routledge, London

Hoggett, B. (1990) "Mental Health Law", Sweet and Maxwell, London

DOH and Welsh Office (1990) "Code of Practice - Mental Health Act 1983", HMSO, London

DOH (1991) "Implementing Community Care: Purchaser, Commissioner and Provider Roles", HMSO, London

DOH (1990) "From Home Help to Home Care"

Eastman, M. (1990) "Old Age Abuse", Age Concern, London

Part Two

Residential Care

Types of Care

There are three basic types of residential care available: local authority care (provided under Part III National Assistance Act 1948); residential care provided by voluntary organisations, and private residential care. There is a further division between residential care homes and nursing homes, broadly based on type and degree of care provided but subject to different registration requirements (see below).

The number of people aged 65 or over living in residential accommodation has grown from 157,193 in 1980 to 235,856 in 1990. This is about 4% of the over-65 population as a whole but 1 in 5 of those over 85. The biggest growth has been in the private sector with 60% of private sector residents being funded from DSS benefits. The burgeoning cost of funding private care through the benefits system has been a major factor in provoking the reassessment of how residential care for older people is to be allocated and funded.

Entry to Residential Care

The decision to enter residential care is more often dictated by circumstances than positive choice. Phillips (1992) found that the key factors were a decline in health and the breakdown of family or community support. However, in terms of the characteristics of those entering residential care there are no great differences to be found between the public, the private and the voluntary sectors except that those entering private care are more likely to be home-owners and less likely to be suffering from mental rather than physical illness.

Entry to local authority residential care is by application to the local authority in whose area the applicant is 'ordinarily resident'. The procedure is by assessment by a social worker as to suitability and need; this 'gatekeeping' function is often backed up by an allocation 'panel' composed of officers of the local authority and other professionals. Waiting lists may apply and it is rare for transfers between homes to be possible, or for out-of-authority applicants to be accepted.

Entry to homes run by voluntary organisations, e.g. Age Concern, is either by direct application or by agency arrangements made with the local authority. Local authorities will be able to supply, on request, lists of registered private homes in their area but the extent to which social workers are able or willing to give advice or actual assistance in choosing a private home varies very much from one authority to another.

Most admissions to private residential care are in fact arranged by relatives (Phillips, 1992). The best procedure is first of all to visit the home and to speak with the proprietor or manager; this gives the resident a chance to see the home and to discuss their care requirements. If a personal visit is not possible, then the home manager should visit the potential resident in their own home or in hospital if that is where he is. The home manager will be conducting his own assessment of the resident's suitability. The next stage is to offer a period of 'short-term care' or a trial period of normally one month before a formal contract is signed giving terms and conditions of residence. It is usual for payment to be required monthly in advance and for four weeks' notice of termination by the resident to be required. Agreeing to the terms of the contract for residential care does not create a tenancy; the legal status of the resident is that of licensee – terminable on 'reasonable notice'.

Registration Requirements

Private residential care homes are required by the Registered Homes Act 1984 to register with the local authority in their area. Nursing homes are registered by the Health Authority under Part II of the same Act, and dual registration is also possible. The legal distinction between residential care homes and nursing homes is based on the type of care provided and the requirement that, in the case of registered nursing homes, qualified nursing staff should be on duty 24 hours a day.

Section 1(1) of the Registered Homes Act defines a residential care home as: "any establishment which provides or is intended to provide, whether for reward or not, residential accommodation with both board and personal care by reason of old age, disablement, past or present dependence on alcohol or drugs, or past or present mental disorder".

All homes must display their current certificate of registration in a conspicuous place in the home and non-registration is a criminal offence. 'Small homes' with fewer than four residents were previously exempt from the registration requirement but, with the passing of the Registered Homes (Amendment) Act 1991, they have been brought within the ambit of the legislation. It may well be that establishments caring for people under adult placement schemes on the 'fostering' model come within the Act.

Both the owner and the manager of the home (if a different person) will need to be registered as both are treated as persons 'carrying on the home'. Registration may be refused if the registration authority is satisfied that any person carrying on the home is not a fit person or the premises are not fit to be used for the purpose of the home or the facilities to be provided are not such as are reasonably required. Registration may also be cancelled on any of the above grounds, if the annual fee is not paid or if any offence under the Act is committed. However, in the case of 'small homes', the 1991 Act stipulates that registration may be refused on only one ground – the 'fit person' ground. Moreover, for small homes the local authority may waive the whole or part of the initial or annual registration fee, though regulations may provide for the making of annual returns to the local authority.

Registration then is some assurance that minimum standards have been met and Schedule 1 of the 1984 Act sets out the information which must be provided when registration is sought. The certificate of registration states the maximum number of persons who may be resident and the registration may also be subject to conditions concerning the age, sex or category of persons who may be admitted. The local authority adopts a 'watchdog' but also an advisory role in relation to homes for which it is responsible. Registration officers have powers of entry at all times and spot checks may be made. It is a criminal offence to obstruct such a person in the execution of his duty. The Residential Care Homes Regulations furthermore provide that proper records should be kept and that every resident should be informed of the person to whom and the manner in which any complaints may be made. However, the role of the local authority is also to provide guidance on meeting standards and sustaining good quality care.

Paying for Residential Care

Local authority homes are required by Section 22 of the Health Service & Public Health Act 1968 to charge what is known as the 'standard rate' for their accommodation. This is the maximum that can be charged and varies from authority to authority; however, when Section 44 of the National Health Service & Community Care Act 1990 is implemented, the standard charge must reflect the full cost to the authority of providing that accommodation. When a person becomes permanently resident in a local authority home, the authority will undertake (with his consent) a full 'financial assessment' taking into account his income, capital and property. Liability to pay is then fixed on a sliding scale according to individual resources between the full 'standard rate' and what is known as the 'minimum charge' (currently calculated at the single person's rate of retirement pension less a personal allowance). The full value of any property is taken into account except in exceptional circumstances usually restricted to elderly or disabled family members continuing to live in the property. If a person does not wish to dispose of his home in order to provide for the costs of care, the local authority may agree to a legal charge being placed on the property enabling them to recoup their money when the property is eventually sold. Interest may be charged. The local authority has the power to include assets disposed of by the resident in anticipation of his move into residential care but only if those assets were disposed of within six months and only if an intention to avoid their inclusion in the assessment can be proved. When Section 21 of the Health and Social Services and Social Adjudication Act 1983 is implemented, assets will be able to be traced into the hands of persons to whom the assets were given.

Particular rules relate to short-term care in local authority homes for the elderly. Often known as 'respite care', this system is frequently used to give carers a break or to serve as recuperation or convalescence for residents themselves. A special 'standard rate' is charged for this type of care, regardless of financial circumstances. Local authorities are empowered to charge this rate for a maximum of eight weeks at any one time. Regular periods of short-term care (sometimes called 'rotating care'), are sometimes a useful way of maintaining people in the community who otherwise would contemplate permanent admission to residential care. Entitlement to Attendance Allowance is not lost provided each period of care lasts no longer than four weeks and those four weeks are separated by at least 28 days.

The financial costs of private residential care are paid directly by residents themselves, except that those with a low income and less than £8,000 capital may apply at present to the DSS for income support to top up their income. The current (1992) maximum per week is £175 for basic residential home fees and £270 for nursing home fees (though higher rates may apply for the very dependent elderly, those who were disabled before the age of 65 or the terminally ill). The value of property is taken into account, except that a period of up to 26 weeks is allowed in order to try to sell the property. During those 26 weeks, benefit will be paid, and the period can be extended at the DSS's discretion. There is no time limit for the inclusion of disposed-of assets among the aggregation of accessible resources. The National Health Service & Community Care Act 1990 will bring about considerable changes in the way in which applicants for publicly funded residential care are supported and assessed. Although existing residents in private residential and nursing homes will continue to be supported through the social security system, all new applicants for public funding after April 1993 will have to apply to the local authority to 'top up' whatever income the applicant has from other sources. In effect, local authorities will 'place' people in private residential homes, after an assessment process designed to identify those applicants who could remain in the community with other forms of support.

The Future of Residential Care

Government policy on residential care, as for other forms of care, is to see the local authority as an enabler rather than a provider, fulfilling its statutory duties by arranging for care in the voluntary and private sectors as well as, or instead of, in its own residential homes. The process by which 'contracting for care' is carried out will therefore assume primary importance.

To offer full choice, the local authority should have contacts with a variety of homes, including nursing homes subject to the requirement that placements in nursing homes will require the consent of the health authority. The local authority would ultimately be responsible if fees were not paid to a private residential home or nursing home with whom it had contracted to provide care. Much emphasis will be placed on quality control and quality assurance; from the point of view of home-owners, however, the local authority will in future need to be very clear about when they are conducting contract compliance evaluations and when they are conducting inspections for registration, as the two are legally quite different.

The Code of Practice known as 'Home Life' has become a standard reference point for the assessment of quality in residential care. Drawing upon these principles, the Department of Health's Social Services Inspectorate has produced new policy guidance for both local authority and home-owners concerned with the registration process. This document called 'Homes are for Living in' (HMSO 1989) aims to provide as it says: "a model for evaluating quality of care provided and quality of life experienced in residential care homes for elderly people." Thus matters such as staffing levels, shared occupancy of rooms and the efficient maintenance of records are not to be seen in isolation but as indicators of the six basic values: Privacy, Dignity, Independence, Choice, Rights and Fulfilment. Thus registered homes have to comply with statute, with regulations and with the local authority's own requirements for quality.

The local authority's ultimate sanction for non-compliance with any of the above is refusal or cancellation of registration, usually after a period of negotiation during which representations may be made. Section 11 of the Registered Homes Act 1984, however, provides for an emergency procedure whereby the local authority may apply for an order from the magistrate's court (or even a single justice of the peace) for the immediate cancellation of registration. The application may be made *ex parte* (that is without notice to the other side).

There is a right of appeal to the Registered Homes Tribunal against a decision of the registration authority to refuse or cancel registration or an order made by a justice of the peace or by a court immediately to cancel registration. An appeal must be lodged within 28 days of the decision appealed against. Decisions of the Registered Homes Tribunal have helped to clarify the interpretation of the law (for a digest of these decisions, see Harman and Harman, 1989). The DSS also keeps a central register of those who have been de-registered under the Act and police checks are now available to disclose past criminal convictions. A conviction, however, under Section 2 of the Act for running an unregistered home is not, it has been decided, an absolute bar to applying for registration in the future.

The National Health Service and Community Care Act 1990 has given an impetus to the creation of inspection units within local authorities with an emphasis on quality assurance. Official guidance on practice for inspection units in SSDs is given in the document 'Inspecting for Quality', 1991. These units deal with complaints procedures under the Act as well as inspection of registered homes. The Social Services Inspectorate has published two documents: Guidance on Standards for Residential Homes for Elderly People; and Guidance on Standards for Residential Homes for People with a Physical Disability, which may be used to set standards for local authority and voluntary care, as well as for private homes. Indeed, both the White Paper on Community Care (1989) and the Policy Guidance (1990) advocate that the so-called 'free standing', i.e. separate from, line management, inspection units should ensure that consistency of standards and approach are applied to public, private and voluntary sectors. In future, therefore, no discrepancy of standards should exist between any of these three sectors. Inspection units are to be supported by an advisory committee in each authority to serve as a forum for the exchange of views between the authority, its officers and service-providers who are subject to inspection or other quality control measures.

Suggestions for further reading

DOH/Caring for People (1991) "Inspecting for Quality. Guidance on Practice for Inspection Units in Social Services Departments and Other Agencies: Principals, Issues and Recommendations", HMSO, London

Phillips, J. (1992) "Private Residential Care: The Admission Process and Reactions of the Public Sector", Avebury, London

Harman, H. and Harman, S. (1989) "No Place Like Home. A Report of the First Ninety-Six Cases of the Registered Homes Tribunal", NALGO

DOH (1989) "Homes are for Living In", HMSO, London

DOH (1990) "Guidance on Standards for Residential Homes for Elderly People", HMSO, London

DOH (1990) "Guidance on Standards for Residential Homes for People with Physical Disability", HMSO, London

Centre for Policy on Ageing (1986) "Home Life"

Part Three

Finance and Business Affairs

Social Security Benefits

There is a range of social security benefits available to older people, both means tested and non-means tested. Further benefits are available to those who are disabled and in need of personal care. The law is extremely complex and the following is intended as a guide only.

Retirement Pensions

Entitlement to a retirement pension is dependent upon having reached pensionable age (60 for women and 65 for men) and fulfilment of the National Insurance contribution conditions. Extra pension is payable if entitlement is deferred for up to 5 years; a contribution record may be protected by credits (e.g. during a period of unemployment), or by 'home responsibilities protection'. An additional pension or graduated pension may be paid on top of the basic pension of £54.15 per week (October 1992). A further 25p per week of basic pension is payable on reaching age 80.

Income Support

Income Support can be claimed in addition by anyone whose weekly income is below what is known as the 'applicable amount'. This amount varies according to the category within which the claimant is placed. Income Support is not available to people who have savings of more than £8,000 or who work 16 hours a week or more. Either one of a couple (husband or wife) may claim.

The single person's rate of Income Support is £42.45 and that for a couple is £66.60 (October 1992). Pensioners, however are entitled to one of three different types of premium: the pensioner premium, the enhanced pensioner premium and the higher pensioner premium. The pensioner premium, is payable to claimants or partners aged 60-74 and the enhanced premium to those aged 75-79. The higher pensioner premium of £20.75 or £29.55 for a couple is paid to all those over 80, or to those over 60 who meet the conditions for the disability premium, i.e. they or their partner are in receipt of Attendance Allowance or Disability Living Allowance or War Pensioners' Mobility Supplement or Invalidity Pension or Severe Disablement Allowance. Those in receipt of the higher pensioner premium may in addition receive the severe disability premium if either they live alone and receive Attendance Allowance, with no one receiving Invalid Care Allowance for looking after them, or they do not live alone but their partner also receives Attendance Allowance or the higher or middle rate of the care component of Disability Living Allowance.

Entitlement to Income Support is reduced after six weeks if either the claimant or their partner goes into hospital.

The Social Fund

The Social Fund is administered by the Department of Social Security to make one-off payments chiefly to people on means-tested benefits; it replaces the previous system of single payments and death grants. For those aged 60 or over, savings of over £1,000 are taken into account. There are discretionary and non-discretionary payments.

Non-discretionary payments are funeral payments (see Part Four of this book) and cold weather payments for those on Income Support. A cold weather payment of £5 can be claimed for each period of seven consecutive days where the average daily temperature is 0°C or less, as announced by the government. There is a right of appeal concerning non-discretionary Social Fund payments to a Social Security Appeal

Tribunal. Local offices of the Benefits Agency cannot impose budgetary limits on such payments.

Non-discretionary Social Fund benefits, however, are limited by local budgets and are subject to internal review, not appeal. There are three types of Social Fund payment: community care grants, budgeting loans and crisis loans. Community care grants are specifically available to help people to remain in the community, or to return to the community from institutional or residential care, or to move to more suitable accommodation. Grants or loans are not available to pay fuel or telephone bills, or for domestic help or housing costs, or for medical, optical or dental items. Loans are repayable from future benefit and the applicant will be assessed for his ability to repay. Crisis loans are available to deal with such disasters as fire and flood and are not restricted to people in receipt of benefit.

Housing Benefit

Housing Benefit is a benefit which is paid towards rent, whether in the local authority or the private sector. Benefit is calculated according to a rebate formula based on net income and capital. The upper capital limit for eligibility is £16,000. Benefit is not available to help with water rates and sewerage charges.

Community Charge Benefit

This is payable to house-owners and tenants and to those living in someone else's home. Each half of a couple will receive separate bills but their entitlement to rebate will be based on their joint incomes and savings, up to a maximum of £16,000.

Benefits for Disabled People and Their Carers

Attendance Allowance

For people of both sexes under the age of 65, Disability Living Allowance and Disability Working Allowance, which each have both care and mobility components, replace the old Attendance

Allowance and Mobility Allowance. Those under 65 who receive Disability Living Allowance may continue to receive it after the age of 65 but the mobility component ceases at age 80.

Attendance Allowance continues for those who make a first claim after the age of 66. Attendance Allowance is paid at a lower or higher rate (sometimes called 'day' or 'night' rates) according to the degree of care needed. Current rates are £28.90 and £43.25 (October 1992). It is paid irrespective of the degree of care actually provided and can equally well be paid to people who have no carer. There is no control on how the money is actually spent. It may be claimed towards the cost of residential care (except in local authority homes).

The lower rate of Attendance Allowance is paid to those who require frequent help during the day with normal bodily functions (e.g. washing, going to the toilet), or have need of continual supervision because of the risk of harm to themselves or others. The higher rate of Attendance Allowance is paid to those who need prolonged (at least 20 minutes) or repeated (at least twice nightly) attention or supervision.

Attendance Allowance may be awarded indefinitely or for a set period. There is a six months 'qualifying' period. However, in the case of persons who are terminally ill there is no qualifying period and Attendance Allowance is available under a special procedure for those whose life expectancy is limited to six months or less. The application, backed up by a doctor's report giving details of the condition, may be made by a person other than the patient, who need not then know of his diagnosis or prognosis.

Invalid Care Allowance

Invalid Care Allowance is a flat rate benefit of £32.55 (October 1992) for carers who are aged over 16 and under 65 and who spend at least 35 hours a week looking after someone who receives Attendance Allowance or the higher or middle rate of the care component of Disability Living Allowance. It is not payable to those who earn more than £40 a week, which includes payments from the person for whom they are caring. Invalid Care Allowance is also taken into account when calculating Retirement Pension or Widow's Pension and is counted as income for the purpose of Income Support, Housing Benefit or Community Charge Benefit. Payment of Invalid Care Allowance will, however, attract them a carer's premium for Income Support and by attracting Home Responsibilities Protection will protect future entitlement to Retirement Pension.

Management

For most of our lives we retain personal control over our own financial and business affairs, signing our own cheques and making our own decisions, however eccentric they may seem to the outside world. If health begins to fail as we get older the management of such matters can become an increasing burden, often spiralling out of control before the magnitude of the problem has been appreciated.

There are three ways in which at least an element of dealing with such matters can be handed over to a third party.

1. Appointeeship
2. Power of Attorney
3. Court of Protection Receivership

The first two involve choice on the part of the person whose affairs are concerned. However, if understanding has generally been lost to such an extent that choice cannot be exercised, then the third option will apply and the Court will make most decisions. The vital points to remember are that the elderly person must trust their agent, and the agent must bear in mind he is handling someone else's money and is accountable to them for its management. Also, any control given over is in relation to business and financial affairs, not the physical person of the individual concerned.

1. Appointeeship

This is a system used by the Department of Social Security whereby National Insurance Retirement Pension and other benefits (e.g. Attendance Allowance, Income Support) are paid on behalf of the claimant to an agreed third party (the appointee). The Department prefers a relative, although it will pay to a friend or professional adviser. It does not like to pay direct to the proprietors of residential or nursing homes, and local authorities tend not to allow their employees (e.g. home carers, wardens of sheltered accommodation) to be named. The claimant has to agree to the third party being appointed, as does the Department, which sends one of its officers to interview both parties, in particular checking on the suitability of the third party to be collecting someone else's benefits. The appointment is indefinite until given up by the appointee or revoked by the claimant or the Department. The appointee undertakes to the Department to pay back overpaid benefits which he receives on the claimant's behalf, and to notify the Department of relevant changes in circumstance. The order books are printed in the name of the appointee, who is the person who signs each week's order and collects it from the Post Office, or signs the Department's form authorising payment into a named bank account at 4 or 13-weekly intervals (this is not possible for Income Support which has to be signed for each week as the claimant or his appointee are re-declaring that financial circumstances have not changed and the means-tested benefit is still rightfully payable).

2. Power of Attorney

This is a document which appoints another or others (the attorney) to act in connection with the affairs of the donor. It is vital that, whatever type of Power of Attorney is selected, the donor has sufficient mental understanding at the time the Power is signed to comprehend the nature of the document and its implications.

If the donor wishes to appoint the attorney for a 'one-off' transaction, such as to sell a property, the short form, 'ordinary' Power of Attorney, should be sufficient. This type of document fails and the attorney has no power and no legal protection once the transaction for which it is to be used has been completed or the donor's mental health has failed so that he no longer understands the actions which his attorney is taking.

If the donor is looking to appoint an attorney to handle everyday transactions indefinitely, be it now or in the future, then the newer 'Enduring Power of Attorney' as created by the Enduring Powers of Attorney Act 1985 and subsequent statutory instruments should be used. The document is in a set wording laid down by statutory instrument which must be followed. It is in three sections, an explanatory first part warning the donor of the implications of entering into the document, a middle part identifying the Power of Attorney as being that of a particular donor with personal details such as name and age and which the donor signs, and the third part being signed by the attorney where he acknowledges the responsibilities which he is taking on and his obligations under the law.

The donor can give 'general power' to his attorney so that it will operate in connection with all financial affairs, or put in any restrictions he likes – not to sell a particular asset or that the attorney can only act under the Power once the donor is no longer mentally capable of managing his affairs.

Whilst the donor has understanding, he directs his attorney's actions – to pay this bill but not that. Once the attorney believes the donor is or is becoming incapable of managing his affairs, then the attorney is legally obliged under the Act to register the Enduring Power of Attorney in the Court of Protection. As the donor no longer understands, he cannot control the attorney's actions and so authorise them. So as to continue to have the authority to handle the donor's affairs, the attorney has to have the protection of registration. The donor and at least three members of his family, as detailed by statute, have to be informed by notice of the application to register. This gives a chance for objections to be raised and the Court to consider the validity of the proceedings. A one-off fee (currently £50) is paid and the attorney's authority is temporarily limited to doing those acts which are necessary to protect the donor's affairs only. If there are no objections or the Court considers any objections raised to be invalid, the Power is registered and the attorney can resume acting under the Power as he had before, but now he reaches the decisions and, if anything controversial arises, he can apply to the Court of Protection for guidance.

As a Power of Attorney is a document created by deed, so it can be revoked by the donor by a simple deed of revocation. The only proviso on this relates to Enduring Powers of Attorney which, although capable of revocation whilst unregistered, cannot be revoked once registered in the Court.

3. Court of Protection – Receivership

If no valid Enduring Power of Attorney has been signed and an individual is unable to manage their affairs because of mental incapacity, then, in order for such matters to be handled properly, there is no option but to apply to the Court of Protection. The Court's authority is found in Sections 93 - 113 of the Mental Health Act 1983.

The Court requires medical evidence (usually from the GP and for which he will charge a fee) on a standard form, that the individual (known as the patient) is incapable so that the Court has jurisdiction. It is worth checking with medical attendants first that any confusion arises from failing mental health (e.g. Alzheimer's Disease) and not from alcohol abuse, adverse reaction to medication or an acute infection which, once diagnosed, can be controlled.

As well as medical evidence, the Court requires a brief factual history of the patient, details of his assets and proposals as to what orders are sought. If there is only a small investment to which access is required, the Court will issue a short form order authorising the release of the funds required.

Where the individual runs his own home, there are several assets, and pensions to collect, the Court needs to make more comprehensive provision for the handling of his affairs. This is done by way of a First General Order which usually appoints a Receiver, a named person, generally a relative, who is authorised to collect all future pensions and income from investments. The First General Order may go on to authorise the rationalisation of assets by the closure of small investments, the disposal of personal chattels, the sale of property and to specify the whereabouts of securities and valuables for safekeeping.

A lay, non-professional Receiver will generally have to be fidelity bonded, taking out an insurance against misappropriation of monies. He will be expected to open a Receivership bank account in his own name 'as Receiver for "the patient"' and is encouraged to have all monies passing through this account. Generally, the Court will require an annual account to be prepared, coinciding with the anniversary of the First General Order and it is much easier to prepare the account if all transactions have gone through the bank. This is also a convenient time to suggest to the Court any changes in policy, reinvestment etc.

The Receiver cannot touch capital unless specifically ordered to. If income is insufficient to meet residential home fees, then an approach is made to the Court for a short order authorising the release of funds from a specific investment of the patient's.

Where assets are jointly owned, bank accounts requiring joint signatures, or the matrimonial home, there can be problems if one of the parties is not capable of comprehending any transaction so that their signature is worthless. The Court has the power to authorise someone else to sign, generally not the capable spouse as there are elements of trust law to be considered, so another, third person is involved to complete the transaction.

The Court has power to make a Statutory Will on behalf of the Patient if he no longer has testamentary capacity and either no will or one sufficiently out of date to require alteration. Having considered evidence of the relatives, assets and the patient's likely views if he could express them, the Court orders the making of a will on the patient's behalf.

There are many misunderstandings about the involvement of the Court of Protection. Whilst the Court is based in London, it is easy to deal with by post and telephone, its staff are helpful and physical appearance in the Court building is rare – generally only if issues are being contested or a will or similar major matter is being considered. Appointments of Receivers, selling properties, agreeing accounts are postal matters. The Court procedure is slow but, if full information is given from the beginning, the Court can carry out its investigations and make its orders reasonably early. If there is an emergency, the Court staff and the Master will do their best to produce an order quickly. It is not cheap: there are Court fees along the way, an annual percentage and legal fees for the work done. All of these come from the patient's assets. Despite this, the affairs have to be properly handled, and it does give everyone peace of mind to know things are being done correctly. Also, if tackled early enough, the proceedings often bring to light the fact that full benefits and tax allowances are not being claimed and that monies can be invested for a better return, so that the increased income generated will often make up for the costs necessarily expended.

One golden rule: approach doctors, social workers and solicitors who are experienced in this type of work and do not be put off by banks and building society staff who do not understand the paperwork with which they will be presented as it will appear unusual.

Lifetime Gifts

In anticipation of moving into permanent care, many elderly people consider giving away the majority of their assets. Before committing themselves to such an irrevocable step, all the implications need to be considered carefully.

By giving his inheritance early, a parent may be giving up the only remaining form of control he has. Once the family have the monies or assets, they may no longer be so willing to visit or fulfil any other obligations. Once a gift is made, it cannot be recalled and, by its nature, no conditions can be imposed.

From an Inheritance Tax "death duty" point of view, such gifts may be ineffective. If, for example, an elderly parent transfers his house into the name of his child but continues to reside in the property, the gift is not tax effective, and will only become so once the parent moves out on a permanent basis.

If the parent is giving away an asset other than their only or main residence, there may be Capital Gains Tax to pay on any increase in value between the date when the asset was originally acquired (or March 1982 if later) and the date of the gift. There is no Capital Gains Tax if assets pass on death.

So far as the child is concerned, there may be a future Capital Gains Tax problem. Any increase in value between the date of gift and subsequent disposal by that child may give rise to a Capital Gains Tax subject to annual allowances etc.

Such gifts are often made in the mistaken belief either that, on going into care, the state takes everything or that, by having no assets, the elderly person will pay minimum fees.

The state does not take anything. It merely expects people to pay the relevant fees for their particular accommodation out of their own resources, as supplemented by relevant benefits.

As far as local authority Part III accommodation is concerned, an assessment is made based on income and means. Fees are levied, up to a possible maximum, based on the ability to pay. The resident has an allowance, uprated every year (currently £10.85 per week), to be used for their personal expenses. If all they have is the state pension, then all that is paid is their pension less the £10.85 allowance. Each year the fees are reassessed to take into account increased charges and pensions, and decreased capital.

If, prior to going into care, the elderly person has given away an asset or assets (generally their home), there are regulations which allow the fact of the gift to be disregarded so that the fees charged are calculated as if the asset was still owned. There are statutory provisions to be brought into force which will allow the local authority to follow the asset to the relative and levy a charge against them for the fees. The rough guideline is that gifts made within the six months prior to entry into care will be counted.

So far as private residential and nursing homes are concerned, they set their own fees and, as long as they are paid, are not concerned where the money comes from. Payment is met by a combination of state benefits and private resources. Many homes set their fees at a level whereby they can be covered by the maximum state benefits available. Again, there is specific provision in the Income Support Regulations for gifts, considered to have been made in order to avoid using one's own capital to pay fees, to be ignored so that the additional help of Income Support is not then paid. Theoretically, gifts made at any time can be ignored if their primary purpose was to try and put the giver into the position whereby the means-tested benefit of Income Support could be paid.

Right to Buy

It is often suggested to elderly people that they take advantage of the right to buy legislation whereby a council tenant for at least two years may be entitled to purchase their home from the council. The longer the term of the tenancy the bigger the discount. The situation often arises whereby older tenants have been in a property so long that they have built up an extremely healthy discount but they do not have sufficient capital even so to pay the discounted purchase price and, being retired and on pensions, inadequate income to meet mortgage payments. Often, younger relatives will suggest that the elderly person takes advantage of the right to buy legislation whilst the younger relative either puts in the capital purchase price or is responsible for the mortgage. Considerable thought must be given by all concerned before entering into this sort of an arrangement. What happens if repairs, etc., are required; who pays? What happens if the younger relative fails to keep up the mortgage payments?

Thought should be given to a Trust Deed behind the actual conveyance when the property is purchased, setting out the exact proportions in which the property is owned, what happens if the elderly person has to go into care and the competing claims of various relatives if one child puts up the capital in order for a property to be purchased whilst others just sit back and hope to benefit from his investment.

Certain sheltered accommodation, or other housing which is regarded as particularly suitable for occupation by the elderly, may not be covered by the right to buy legislation because it is felt that councils should have available housing stock providing for special needs. (See Part One)

It also has to be borne in mind that any property sold within three years of the right to buy legislation may be subject to claw-back, so that some of the discount available at the time of purchase is reclaimed by the council on sale.

Moving in with relatives

If relatives move in with each other, be it to take advantage of the right to buy legislation, to build on an annexe or to buy a custom-built property with additional facilities for the elderly relative, again great care must be taken before such an arrangement is entered into. It should be carefully planned in advance where the money is coming from and in what proportion. If the mortgage is unpaid, the elderly person could find themselves homeless and without any automatic recourse to council accommodation. What if the arrangement falls apart, how does everyone get their money out? What if the elderly person has to go into care, again they may need their money back to pay fees. What happens on the death of any of the participants in this arrangement? A much higher proportion than people realise, of these arrangements collapse or experience difficulties. Just because the arrangement is within the family, there is no reason to suppose that it will not experience difficulties and that it need not be committed to a clear written understanding.

Home Income Plans

It is possible to raise capital from one's own property by way of a Home Income Plan or Home Reversion Plan. This is an arrangement whereby either a mortgage is taken out on the property or the property itself is sold and the capital received as a result is used to purchase an annuity (and sometimes to provide a little bit of fall-back capital) so as to effectively increase income. These need to be considered with extreme care and professional and independent advice need to be taken at an early stage. The increase in income may well mean a reduction in eligibility for benefits such as Income Support and Community Charge Benefit so that, once careful sums have been done, many of the people most interested in such schemes find that, financially, they are not practical.

Suggestions for further reading

Letts, P. (1990) "Handling Other People's Money", Age Concern

"Your Rights - A Guide to Money Benefits for Older People", (Published annually), Age Concern

"Enduring Powers of Attorney", An Explanatory Booklet (Free), Public Trust Office Leaflets

"When I'm Sixty-Five", (Free), The Law Society

"Using your Home as Capital", Age Concern

Part Four

Death and Family Provision

Death

Having organised one's business affairs through life, it is equally important to ensure that clear arrangements are made to deal with such matters on death. There are many popular misconceptions about who gets what and how the system works.

Whatever the position in life, all management arrangements cease on death. An attorney's authority automatically ends, a Court of Protection Receivership ceases (save for the formal winding-up of the Court proceedings) and assets and liabilities become the responsibility of the duly constituted personal representatives. Arguments that "I am the next-of-kin" are irrelevant.

Funeral Arrangements

Disposal of the body is the immediate problem. If the coroner is involved, as he will be in sudden or unexpected deaths, then the body is subject to his jurisdiction and no funeral can be held until he agrees to release it, having been satisfied that it is not needed for further tests, etc. Strictly, the funeral arrangements should be the responsibility of the executors if there is a will. Often, family or friends make the arrangements and then tell the executors; however, they should not be surprised if some professional executors react starchily to arrangements to which they have not been a party. As a matter of contract law, the person who makes the arrangements with the funeral director is the one who is responsible for payment of the bill – the contract is between those two parties. If the estate does not pay up, the funeral director will come after whoever made the arrangements for payment. If there is little money, or likely to be problems, do not get involved. In the former case, the DSS may pick up the bill if the deceased had few assets but only if the person making the arrangements is on Income Support, Family Credit, Housing Benefit or Community Charge Benefit. Even so, any assets which there may be in the estate are looked to in order to repay the DSS's outlay.

The death has to be registered before the funeral can take place. If the coroner is involved, it can be registered afterwards if the coroner has authorised the funeral and there is no inquest, or it is done automatically after any inquest verdict. Registration must be done by the closest available kin; if there is no kin, whoever is arranging the funeral or the householder of the premises where the death took place, may find themselves involved.

Distribution of Estate

Most joint assets can be transferred fairly easily to the surviving co-owner or owners simply on production of a death certificate. That is because the property is held on what is known as a 'joint tenancy' whereby the property passes automatically to the surviving co-owner or owners. Assets held this way cannot be controlled by will as, by operation of law, the document controlling the joint ownership is the conveyance on house purchase or application form to open an account and it takes precedence over the dispositions in a will.

One exception to this is where land is owned by co-owners on a 'tenancy in common' basis. In that instance, the surviving co-owners have the title in their names and can dispose of it (although one surviving co-owner will have to appoint a second person as trustee before a purchaser will pay over the purchase price) but the land is held for the estate of the deceased co-owner and the survivors in the relevant proportions upon which it was originally held. A tenancy in common can be applied to other assets but banks and building societies have difficulty recognising the concept in practice.

Assets in the sole name of the deceased become temporarily frozen once the death certificate is produced. It is for the personal representatives to deal with these assets once they can establish their right so to do. The broad guideline is that if the total estate is worth over £5,000 then either Probate or Letters of Administration (a Grant of Representation) is needed: if the estate value is less than £5,000 then neither is necessary. Even so, it can sometimes work out simpler, and marginally cheaper in practice, to obtain Probate or Letters of Administration for a small estate if there are several tiny assets in different places; the Grant of Representation is universally acceptable, whereas each bank, building society or insurance company has its own slightly different procedure when no Grant is available.

A will should ensure that the deceased's wishes are carried out and those whom the deceased wished to benefit receive their due. The will must conform with the formalities of the Wills Act 1837 (as amended), for example that it is in writing, signed, and witnessed by two independent witnesses and that all three signatures take place together and in the right order.

Although it is tempting to try writing out one's will oneself, or buying a will form from a stationer, some of the formalities are often missed out and the 'will' fails and so has no legal effect. This is often not discovered until after the person has died, by which time it is too late to rectify the mistakes unless everyone involved is prepared to agree.

Most wills, if professionally drawn, are certainly not expensive relative to the overall value of the estate and the importance of directing the inheritance to the right place. For some small estates it may be possible for people over the age of 70 to make wills n Legal Aid using the Green Form (instant advice) scheme.

If there is no will, the estate is distributed according to set rules laid down by the Administration of Estates Act 1925 and subsequent statutory instrument. Everything does not automatically pass to a surviving spouse, or to the eldest son on the death of both or the second parent. In each case, both the size of the deceased's estate and the classes of relatives they have left are considered.

If there is a spouse and no children, the spouse inherits personal chattels, the first £125,000 and half the rest of the estate over £125,000. The other half passes to the deceased's other relatives, for example parents or brothers and sisters.

If there is a spouse and children of the deceased, then the surviving spouse receives personal chattels, the first £75,000 and the income only from half the estate over £75,000. The other half passes immediately to the deceased's children at age 18, as does the first half on the death of the surviving spouse.

If there is no spouse, the whole estate is distributed amongst all members of the nearest class of relatives to the deceased, beginning with children or other issue; if there are no children then it falls to parents, then brothers and sisters and so on. If having looked as far as cousins, there are no relatives, the entire estate can end up going to the state (i.e. going into government coffers).

Family Provision

It is always open to persons who feel that the deceased has not provided for them adequately to contest the will or operation of the intestacy rules by suing the estate under The Inheritance (Provision for Family and Dependents) Act 1975. To bring a successful action, the claimant must come within one of five classes of people able to sue, spouses, ex-spouses, children, children of a marriage (basically step-children) and any other person. This last class is most commonly used by surviving partners of a non-marital relationship but can be used by others. In addition, the claimant must show some form of dependency, e.g. if an adult child, making his own way in the world challenges a parent's will that leaves everything to charity, he will most certainly not succeed.

Often one spouse will make a will cutting out or restricting the inheritance of their partner who is in care, in the belief that the state system will fund them. There is a suggestion that local authorities and the DSS will encourage such surviving spouses to bring actions under this Act on the basis that they have not been provided for adequately. Only time will tell how much this provision will be used, but families should be aware of the potential difficulties if one spouse makes a will totally cutting out their partner on that partner's admission into permanent residential care which is heavily subsidised by the state.

Taxation

No Capital Gains Tax is payable on death. The death duty tax is Inheritance Tax. Gifts between husband and wife (but not co-habitees) are exempt from tax, unless the receiving spouse is non-UK domiciled, so that any amount can pass from one to the other, tax free. Gifts to charities are also exempt.

Subject to reliefs for business or agricultural property, tax is paid after the first £150,000 at a flat rate of 40%. The size of the estate is calculated by looking at the assets left on death, those given away in the last seven years immediately preceding death and any trust funds in which the deceased had a right to income. Debts, funeral bills, etc. are deducted, and the resultant net figure is the taxable estate.

It is possible to save tax by husband and wife equalising their estates – seeing they each have assets of roughly equivalent value – and then making gifts down to the next generation on the first death, rather than leaving it all to the survivor. It is worth taking professional advice to ensure the correct steps are taken.

After death, deeds of variation can be entered into, altering the dispositions of a will or the operation of the intestacy rules. These are often done for tax-saving purposes and, as long as everyone agrees, the document is written and within two years of death, it should be acceptable to the Inland Revenue. However, it is better to have planned beforehand than to rely on a post-death variation to save the day.

Suggestions for further reading

IRI Inheritance Tax, Capital Taxes Office, Minford House, Rockley Road, London, W14 ODF

"What to do after a death", DSS leaflet D49

"What to do when someone dies", Consumers Association

Appendix

Elderly People's Welfare Organisations

Reference addresses for carers and professionals

Advocacy Alliance
2nd Floor
115 Golden Lane
London
EC1Y OTS

Age Concern England
Astral House
1268 London Road
London
SW16 4ER   Tel: 081 679 8000

Alzheimers Disease Society
158-160 Balham High Road
London
SW12 9BN   Tel: 081 675 6557

Arthritis Care
5 Grosvenor Crescent
London
SW1X 7ER   Tel: 071 235 0902

Association of Crossroads Care Attendant Schemes Ltd
10 Regents Place
Rugby
Warwickshire
CV21 2PN   Tel: 0788 573653
(To enable disabled people to live at home in the community through home-based
care attendants)

British Association of the Hard of Hearing
7-11 Armstrong Road
London
W3 7JL   Tel: 081 743 1110

BASE – British Association for Service to the Elderly
119 Hassell Street
Newcastle-under-Lyme
Staffs
ST5 1AX   Tel: 0782 661033

British Geriatric Society
1 St Andrew's Place
London
NW1 4LB

British Pensioners' and Trades' Union Action Association
Norman Dodd's House
315 Bexley Road
Erith
Kent
DA8 3EZ   Tel: 0322 335464

Carers' National Association
29 Chilworth Mews
London
W2 3RG   Tel: 071 7247776

Chest, Heart & Stroke Association, Volunteer Stroke Scheme
Manor Farm
Appleton
Abingdon
Oxon
OX13 5JB   Tel: 0865 862954

Contact
15 Henrietta Street
Covent Garden
London
WC2E 8QH   Tel: 071 240 0630
(Companionship and outings for isolated elderly people)

Diabetic Association
10 Queen Anne Street
London
W1M 0BD   Tel: 071 323 1531

Disability Alliance
1st Floor East

Universal House
85-94 Wentworth Street
London
E17 SA   Tel: 071 247 8776

Help the Aged
St James' Walk
London
EC1R OBE   Tel: 071 253 0253

MIND (National Association for Mental Health)
22 Harley Street
London
W1N 2ED   Tel: 071 637 0741

National Trust for the Welfare of the Elderly
Kauri House
33 Hook Road
Goole
North Humberside
DN14 5JB   Tel: 0405 763149

RNIB - Royal National Institute for the Blind
234 Great Portland Street
London
W1N 6AA   Tel: 071 388 1266

Success after Sixty
40/41 Old Bond Street
London
W1X 3AF   Tel: 071 629 0672

Support for the Elderly Mentally Infirm (SEMI)
University Settlement
43 Ducie Road
Barton Mill
Bristol
BS5 OAX   Tel: 0272 559219

WRVS - Women's Royal Voluntary Service
234-244 Stockwell Road
London
SW9 9SP   Tel: 071 416 0146

Index

63